How?

A DRAGON Question Book™

By Kathie Billingslea Smith
Illustrated by Robert S. Storms

A DRAGON BOOK

GRANADA

How long do

Scientists do not agree on exactly how long different animals live. But they do know that some animals have short lives and other animals live for a long, long time.

Most dogs live to be about 13 years old. Horses usually live to be anywhere from 20 to 30 years old.

animals live?

Tortoises have the longest lives of all. Under good conditions, they can live for 100 or more years!

People live to be about 72 years old.

Look at this chart to see how long some other animals live, and people too!

ANIMALS	Average Number of years they live in captivity
mouse	2
rabbit	5
chicken	12
dog	13
cat	14
horse lion	23
cow pig bear	25
camel	40
whale	55
elephant	60
People	72
Land tortoise	100+

How high is the sky?

Many people think that the sky is like a big, blue blanket stretched around the earth. But that is wrong. There is no one place that can be called the sky.

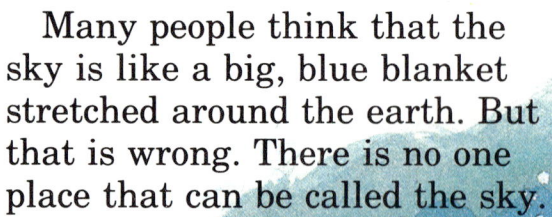

Our earth is really surrounded by an enormous layer of air. It is called the atmosphere. The atmosphere gives us air to breathe and

keeps us from getting too much heat from the sun.

Astronauts out in space can look back at the earth and see the atmosphere. It looks like a blue haze.

When you look up at the sky, you are really looking out into space through the miles and miles of air that make up the atmosphere.

How can we tell the

As trees grow bigger and taller, new layers of wood grow underneath the bark. The wood that is added in the earlier, cold part of the year is a different colour to the wood that grows later in the summer. These rings of different coloured wood make it easy to see how many years a tree has been growing. This is how it works:

When a tree is cut across, you can see a number of rings, one inside the other. Each ring is about one year's growth.

A young tree...

age of a tree?

A 20-year-old tree...

A very old tree...

If a tree has 20 rings, it is about 20 years old. A tree with 60 rings is about 60 years old.

Of course, a tree must be cut down before you can see the rings. To tell the age of a tree that is still standing, you must guess by looking at how big and tall it is. The wider the trunk and the taller the tree, the older the tree is.

How do spiders

Spiders spin their webs with thin threads of silk that are made inside their bodies. The silk comes out of special tubes called spinnerets. Some of the threads are sticky, some are not.

spin their webs?

Different spiders spin different kinds of webs. There are *orb*, or round webs, *triangle* webs, *tangled* webs, and *funnel* webs.

Spiders spin webs as traps to catch food to eat. Insects get caught on the sticky threads of the web. Then the spiders kill the insects and eat them.

Special coatings of oil on the spiders' bodies keep them from sticking to their own webs.

How do injections help

When the doctor gives you an injection, it hurts. But getting one is really worth it because they help you to stay healthy.

Inside your body, blood moves through veins and arteries to every part of you. Your blood is made up of red cells and white cells. Red cells carry oxygen to all parts of your body, helping to keep you alive. The white cells fight bad germs that could make you sick.

Doctors give you injections to help your white cells to kill germs. The injections are full of weak germs that can't hurt you. The weak germs "wake up" your

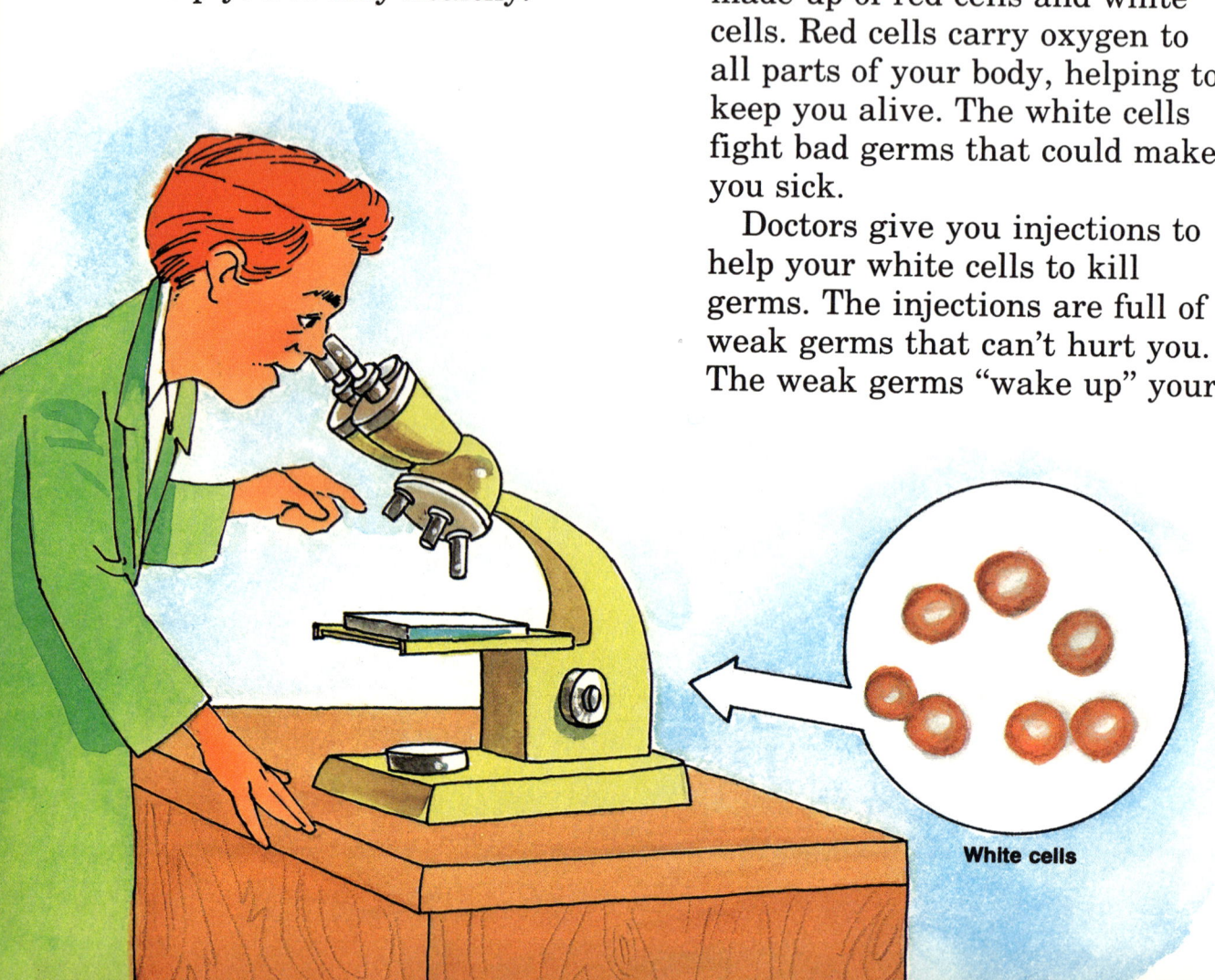

White cells

...me stay healthy?

white cells to make special chemicals to fight these new invading germs. The chemicals are called antibodies. Antibodies kill the weak germs in the shot. Then the antibodies stay in your body to fight off any of these same germs if ever they come again.

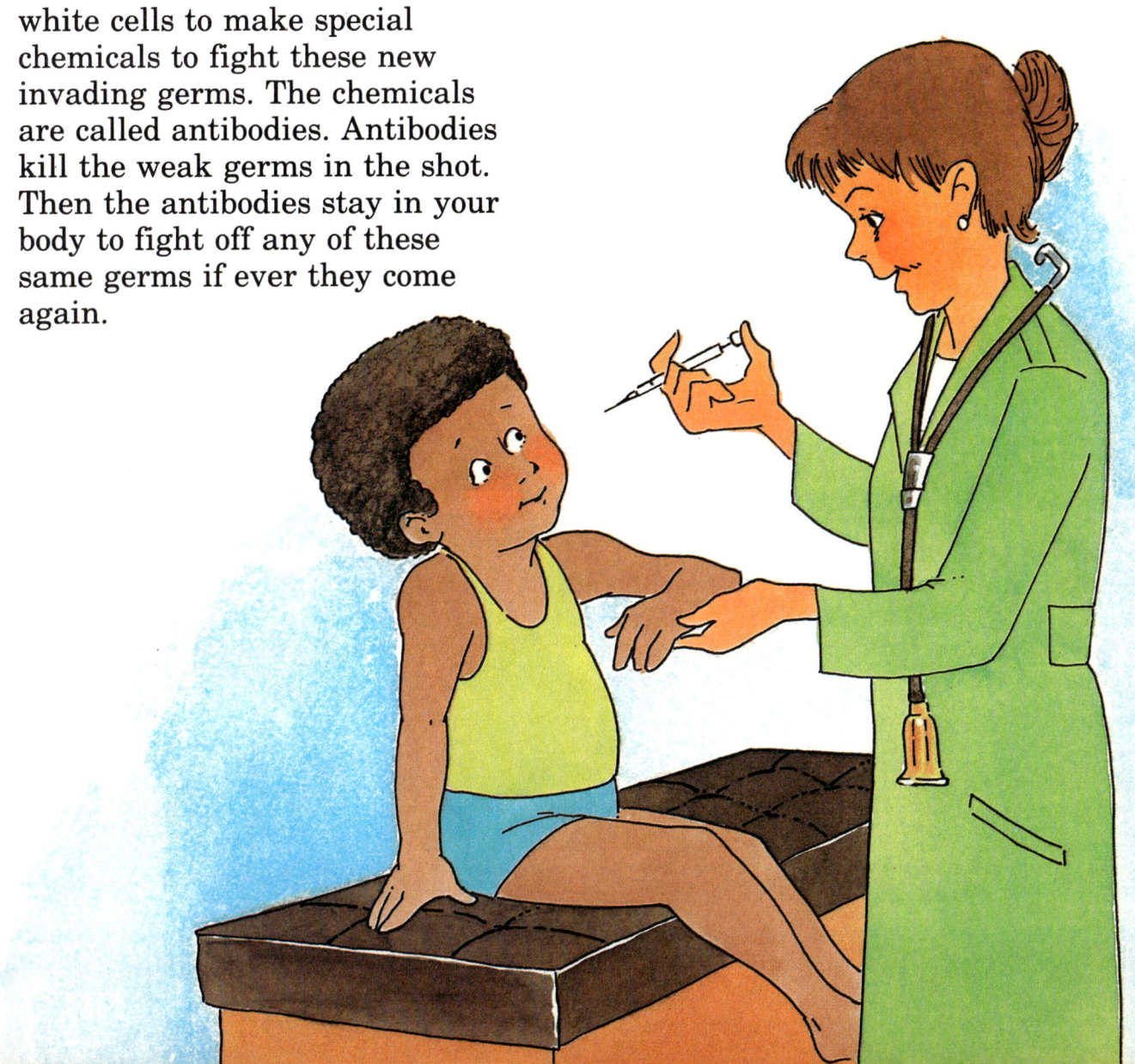

How do blind

Blind people cannot see. They cannot look at pictures or read words printed in books. So they read another way — with their fingers!

A special kind of alphabet is used by blind people. It is called Braille. In Braille, each letter of the alphabet is a special pattern of bumps or dots. They stick up on the pages of Braille books.

eople read?

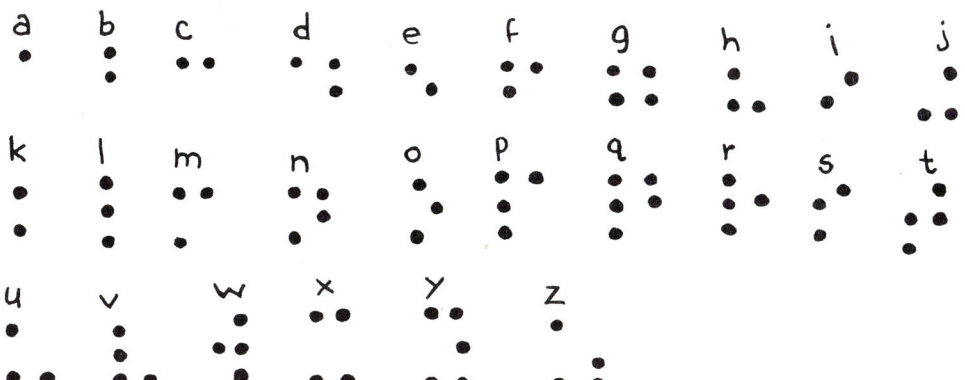

Blind people feel the bumps with their fingers. They have learned what the bumps mean. As they move their fingers over the words written in Braille, they can read almost as quickly as other people can read with their eyes.

Here are the patterns of dots that make up the Braille alphabet:

Can you write your name in Braille?

How big were the

Diplodocus (dih-PLOD-uh-kuss) was the longest dinosaur that ever lived. With its very long neck and tail, Diplodocus grew to be about 28 m long. It was as long as three school buses parked in front of each other. Diplodocus was a plant-eater and had a very small head. Scientists think it must have eaten all day long to take in enough food to feed its huge body.

biggest dinosaurs?

The giant of all dinosaurs was Brachiosaurus (bray-key-uh-SORE-us). This dinosaur was not as long as Diplodocus, but it was the heaviest land animal that ever lived. Brachiosaurus weighed about 79 tonnes.

This is as much as 3,000 children would weigh all together! Brachiosaurus was so heavy that it could hardly move on land and spent most of its time in the water. It could hold its head up high in the air. If Brachiosaurus was alive today, it could rest its head on the roof of a three-storey apartment building!

How do fish

Just like people, fish need oxygen to stay alive. Oxygen is a gas that is found in the air and in water. People breathe oxygen from the air. But fish use their gills to get their oxygen from the water.

breathe underwater?

First the fish open their mouths to let in some water. Then as they close their mouths, the water is pushed between their gills. The blood inside the gills takes the oxygen from the water. This oxygen is carried, by the blood, all through the fishes' bodies. The extra water goes out through the gill openings.

The next time you see some fish, look at them closely and watch them breathe through their gills.

Oxygen in water

Extra water leaves through the gills.

How much is one million?

One million is a very, very large number. It is written like this:

One million is a thousand thousands.

It is hard to imagine just how much one million is.

If you tried to count to one million and said one number every second, without taking time to eat or sleep or play, you would have to count for 11½ days, without stopping!

Suppose you had $1,000,000 to spend. (Wouldn't that be fun?) If you spent one dollar every minute around the clock day and night, it would take you about two years to spend all the money!

Yes, one million is a very, very large number! Think about it.

How did people tell time

the shadow moves from one mark to the next on the plate, telling what hour it is. Sundials were helpful, but they could not be used on cloudy days or at night, because there weren't any shadows then!

Some people burned candle clocks and rope clocks to tell

Long ago, many people used sundials to help them tell time. Sundials are flat, circular plates marked off into hours. A metal stick, called a gnomon, points toward the North Pole. When the sun shines on the sundial, the gnomon makes a shadow on the plate. As the earth turns,

before there were clocks?

time. Painted bands marked the hours on the candle clocks. Rope clocks had knots tied on them for each hour. The number of bands or knots burned away told how many hours had passed.

People also used hourglasses to tell time. An hourglass has a funny shape. Sand falls from the top to the bottom. This takes one hour. Then the hourglass is turned upside down once more.

Today we have clocks and wristwatches to tell the time. They are easy to use and almost work by themselves — in any weather!

How do I remember

You remember many things. You have learned the alphabet and many stories and songs. You know the names of your friends and where they live. You remember how to play different games and what presents you got for your birthday last year.

things?

All of these memories, and others that you have forgotten, are stored inside your brain. Your eyes and ears pick up information and send it to your brain. There are millions and millions of nerve cells there. The information is saved in these cells until you need to remember it.

Many of our memories are forgotten after a few minutes. If you read a story once, you will not remember much of it. But if you read a story over and over, you will remember it for a long time. The more often you study something, the longer you will remember it.

Your brain is always ready to hold new thoughts and ideas. What new things did you learn today?

How tall is the tallest animal?

The tallest animal on earth is the giraffe. Female giraffes grow to be about 4½ metres tall, and male giraffes usually reach a height of 5 metres! That is as tall as a two-storey house!

Giraffes live in small groups on the grasslands of Africa. They use their long necks and legs to eat tasty leaves and twigs from the tops of acacia trees.

It doesn't seem possible, but giraffes' long necks have the same number of *vertebrae*, or bone pieces, that our necks do! The seven vertebrae in the giraffes' necks are simply much longer than ours are.